Nicholas Breakspear
The Pope from England

Simon Webb

© 2016 Simon Webb. The right of Simon Webb to be identified as the Author of the Work has been asserted by him in accordance with the Copyright, Designs and Patents Act 1988. All rights reserved.

This edition published by
The Langley Press, 2016

The cover shows part of an engraving of Nicholas Breakspear from the British Museum

Also from the Langley Press

In Search of St Alban

The Legend of St Alban

The Legend of St Cuthbert

Bede's Life of St Cuthbert

In Search of the Northern Saints

Aaron of Lincoln

The Voyage of St Brendan

Gilbert's Tale: The Life and Death
of Thomas Becket

for free downloads and more from the Langley
Press, visit our website at:

http://tinyurl.com/lpdirect

Contents

Introduction	7
I. The Failed Monk	13
II. The Poor Scholar	19
III. The Abbot	22
IV. Cardinal-Bishop and Legate	29
V. The Leonine City	34
VI. Barbarossa	45
VII. William the Bad	52
VIII. Henry II	57
IX. Barbarossa Returns	63
X. Pope and Anti-Pope	69
XI. Conclusion: John of Salisbury	73
XII. Chronology	79
XIII. Bibliography	82

'I too hope in this short reign to
 be a man of peace.'

Pope Benedict XVI

Pope Adrian IV, from *The Lives and Times of the Popes* by Artaud de Montor, 1911

Introduction

The modern procedure for the election of a new pope demands absolute secrecy: the cardinal-electors make their deliberations behind locked doors, and while the world is permitted to know hardly anything about what they are doing, they in turn are not allowed to know what is going on in the outside world.

Vatican-watchers have to content themselves with looking for smoke from one of the Vatican chimneys. If there is smoke, then a round of voting has been completed and the ballot papers are being burned. If the smoke is white, a pope has been elected. If the smoke is black, then more voting will be needed.

This secret procedure was first introduced to eliminate outside meddling in the business of papal elections. In earlier centuries, the election of a pope, and much of his pontificate, could be affected by interference from powerful individuals outside the church. This made for a very different atmosphere around the papacy, but then in earlier centuries the papacy itself was very different from what it is today.

Every time a pope dies, or retires, and a new one has to be elected, the media in Britain look for possible British candidates. This speculation seems less fanciful since the Polish Cardinal Karol Wojtyła became Pope John Paul II in 1978. John Paul was not just the first Polish pope and the first pope from one of the Slavic countries – he was also the first non-Italian to ascend the throne of St Peter for over four hundred and fifty years. The first Polish pope was succeeded by the seventh German one, Joseph Ratzinger (Pope Benedict XVI), then the first ever Argentine one, so the non-Italian pattern now seems to be established. Could England be next? England is not officially a Roman Catholic country, but then large parts of Germany are not Catholic either.

It is true that of the roughly two hundred and sixty-four popes whose nationalities are known, two hundred and nine were Italians, which is nearly eighty percent; but the Greeks, Germans, Syrians, Africans, Spaniards and Dalmatians who make up another eighteen percent are a reminder that popes don't have to come from Italy. The remainder are from places that have supplied only one pope each: Holland, Poland, Portugal, Palestine (St Peter himself) and England - home of Nicholas Breakspear.

Accounts of the 'popess', Pope Joan, say that she also came from England, but although these stories were widely believed for over two hundred years, they are now regarded as apocryphal. The female pope, who is sometimes called not Joan, but Agnes or Gilberta, is supposed to have posed as a man, giving herself the name Johannes Anglicus or 'John of England'.

In her manly disguise she travelled with her lover, a Benedictine monk, to Athens, where she obtained a first-rate education. In Rome, she became a papal notary and was elected pope in 855, taking the name of John VIII. She is supposed to have reigned for over two years, after the pontificate of Pope Leo IV and before that of Benedict III. Historians now believe that there was an interregnum of only a few weeks between these popes, and that there really isn't enough of a gap in papal history to allow Joan to have reigned.

Joan is supposed to have given the game away by going into labour during a public procession in Rome. Some versions of the legend say the baby was still-born, and that Joan was immediately dragged out of the city and stoned to death. The less bloodthirsty version has it that the popess retired to a nunnery with her living baby.

It used to be believed that the street where Joan's labour started was always avoided by papal processions because of the scandal of what had happened there. There was also a theory that there was a special chair in Rome that any candidate for the papacy had to sit on. The chair was so constructed that the future pope could be examined, and his gender confirmed. In fact the existence of this chair with a strategic hole in it is well-attested, but its purpose is misunderstood. Like much in medieval Rome, the chair was a re-used Ancient Roman artefact – in this case a chair for a wealthy Roman to sit on on after a visit to the bath. The hole was there to allow the bath-water to drain away, and to prevent the chair's owner sitting in a pool of water. Some now believe that the strange design of this chair, which was sometimes used by the popes on public occasions, contributed to the creation of the story of Pope Joan. This is the chair, people guessed, that the cardinals introduced so that there would never be another Pope Joan.

Joan can be eliminated as the first English pope, not least because, although she is supposed to have reigned in the ninth century, she is not mentioned by chroniclers until the thirteenth. That leaves the twelfth-century pope, Breakspear, as the only English pontiff so far. When the question of the papal election comes up, newspapers in Britain will sometimes remind us that there was once a real English pope, but few facts about this remarkable man are offered. To a large extent, the English have forgotten their very own pope.

After Henry VIII's sixteenth-century Reformation, many English people turned their backs on their Roman Catholic heritage, later removing or defacing what were seen as the more 'popish' aspects of their church architecture, and regarding the Bishop of Rome as an enemy – even as the Antichrist. The proud memory of an English pope had little place in a country that had just become Protestant. *Foxe's Book of Martyrs*, the quintessential sixteenth-century Protestant text, characterised Breakspear as a wicked pain in the neck for the German emperor, Frederick I. Foxe tells us, 'much trouble had good Fridericus with this Pope'.

In the diverse, tolerant, open-minded England of the twenty-first century, we are more likely to laugh at the rabid anti-Catholicism of John Foxe than to be inspired by it, and many of us would like to rediscover the ancient Catholic dimension of English religious history, albeit on our own terms.

Nicholas Breakspear, who took the name Adrian (or Hadrian) IV on his election, stands with Chaucer, Thomas More, Shakespeare, GK Chesterton, Graham Greene, Alexander Pope, Edward Elgar and many others in the English Catholic Hall of Fame, but detailed information about him is not easy to find outside academic libraries. The last full-length book about Adrian IV to be published in English appeared in 2003: this volume, edited by Brenda Bolton and Anne J. Duggan, is expensive, scholarly and not intended for a general readership; it is not a narrative of Breakspear's life, but rather a collection of essays and sources.

Before the 2003 book, there were others

published in 1925, 1907 and 1905. These, and the handful of studies brought out in the nineteenth century, are now hard to come by, and are of course lacking the insights and discoveries of modern scholars.

Breakspear was not a particularly great or saintly pope, but he was a gifted and interesting man who 'lived in interesting times', to paraphrase an old Chinese curse. This book is intended as a straightforward, impartial account of his life and times.

I. The Failed Monk

Some time around the year 1115, a certain young man had a very important interview with the bishop of St Albans in Hertfordshire. At the interview, the abbot was to tell the young man whether he would be accepted as a monk in this large, prestigious abbey. Unfortunately (or perhaps fortunately as things turned out) the abbot told the young man that he could not be accepted straight away, and advised him to 'Have patience, my son, and stay at school yet a while till you are better fitted for the position you desire'.

He could not have been aware of it at the time, but the abbot had just caused one of the most remarkable false-starts in history. He had rejected Nicholas Breakspear; future scholar, monk, abbot, cardinal, papal legate and, ultimately, pope.

We don't know exactly when Nicholas's interview with the abbot happened, and we don't even know for certain when Breakspear was born, so we can't say if he was really too young when he met with the abbot, or if the abbot had some other objection to Nicholas, and was using his age as an excuse to reject him. If this was the case, then it may be that the abbot thought Nicholas was needed at home, to generate income for his family, which was apparently very poor. Of course, if the family was living in poverty, then Nicholas may not have had enough education to be accepted as a novice monk.

The story of Nicholas's rejection at St Albans comes to us via Matthew Paris, a thirteenth-century historian who was himself a monk at St Albans. Paris, who was also an illuminator of manuscripts, was not always a slave to the truth, and he might have made up the rejection story to smooth out some narrative bumps in Breakspear's biography. How else could he account for the fact that Breakspear hadn't been a monk at St Albans? As well as this possible 'tweaking' or artistic licence, there are other serious holes in Matthew Paris's story – for instance, Paris calls the abbot in question Robert, but there was no Robert in that position at St Albans until much later, in 1151.

Fortunately Matthew Paris, who is known to have been (at times) both a careless and an over-inventive historian, is not our only early source of information on Nicholas Breakspear. Others include Cardinal Boso, who probably wrote his *Life of Adrian IV* in the 1170s. Boso was a close associate of Breakspear as pope, and as papal chamberlain had a lot of responsibility for the day-to-day running of the papal states. Other sources include chronicles from Germany, Ireland and

England, and a Latin verse biography of Breakspear's old sparring-partner, Frederick Barbarossa.

Nicholas Breakspear was born around 1100, and is thought to have lived at Abbot's Langley in Hertfordshire, a village which is just a few miles from St Albans itself. His surname is a very rare and ancient one among the English, and it is supposed to be a prestigious name, as it suggests that his first ancestor to be called 'Breakspear' broke the lance or 'spear' of his opponent in a jousting match. As only rich men could afford the horses, armour, lances and other equipment needed for the dangerous and expensive sport of jousting, the surname 'Breakspear' suggests aristocratic roots.

If Breakspear's ancestry was really noble, then the career of his father suggests that the family had come down in the world. Richard Breakspear was a poor priest and monk of St Albans. We don't know if Richard was both a priest and monk when he fathered his famous son – if he was, then Nicholas was technically illegitimate. If, on the other hand, Richard Breakspear was a cleric in minor orders when he fathered Nicholas, then he would have been entitled to be married and to have children.

It is certain that Richard became a monk of St Albans at some point. If he had entered the cloister after his worldly responsibilities had all slipped away – perhaps after his wife died and when his children were already making their way in the world, then his choice of the monk's cowl can be seen as praiseworthy. But according to William of Newburgh, who wrote about Nicholas at the end of the twelfth century, Breakspear's father left his family in poverty when he became a monk.

Even if he wasn't cursed with a negligent absentee father, Nicholas's childhood as a poor boy in Norman England is likely to have been pretty dire. Thirty-five years before Nicholas was born, the Normans invaded England from France. At the famous Battle of Hastings, William of Normandy earned his nickname of Conqueror by defeating King Harold and his Anglo-Saxon army. The Normans went on to subdue England, to build castles all over it, to place foreigners in all the top jobs and to squeeze the poor natives for taxes until the pips squeaked. The culture of the Anglo-Saxons was quickly replaced by the new Norman culture, and Saxon names like Aethelfrith and Osric were cast aside in favour of French ones like William and Robert.

The English suddenly found themselves with a French-speaking ruling class who were addicted to building vast stone churches and monasteries. St Albans Abbey is one of the great monasteries the Normans started, although Christianity in this Hertfordshire city goes back to Roman times. The Romans called the city Verulamium: its modern name commemorates the first English Christian martyr, who was executed there in the third or fourth century.

In Nicholas's day the abbey and its church dwarfed the ancient city itself, which was narrow and mean by comparison. For a poor boy from a small village the abbey (which was brand new, having only been completed in 1115) must have looked like the heavenly Jerusalem described in the Biblical Book of Revelation:

'And the building of the wall of it was of jasper: and the city was pure gold, like unto clear glass.' Rev. 21:18, KJV

This particular version of paradise was, as we know, closed to the boy from Abbot's Langley. At home, Nicholas had to get over his rejection at the hands of the abbot of St Albans, and consider his options. Should he wait, and return to St Albans after a couple of years as the abbot had suggested? Should he try another English monastery? Should he give up his hopes of the religious life altogether and live as a peasant?

If Breakspear had chosen the life of a poor commoner in those times (assuming that this station in life had been open to him) then his years would have been hard, and probably short in number. Many country people living under the Normans came home to nothing better than a 'cruck' house, a sort of low tent of wood, covered in turf to keep in the warmth and to keep out the weather. Here the occupants would live with their animals in cramped, filthy, smoky conditions.

If Breakspear the peasant had married, his wife would probably have had a baby a year, many of which children would have died in infancy. His work on the land would have been back-breaking and unrewarding, his diet poor and, when it was not scarce, monotonous. He would have been a saint not to have cursed the name of the abbot who had rejected him. All his life, he would have envied the relatively secure and comfortable lives of the monks.

Things were tough for the monks too – they were forced to rise at all hours of the night to attend services, and their food was often plain and limited. But they had the chance of an education – a window into a wider world of history and spirituality, of languages, literature, art, architecture and sacred music. They were not expected to die in wars for their monarch, and they avoided the heartache of family life lived in the constant fear of starvation.

II. The Poor Scholar

Nicholas did not choose the life of a peasant or a monk, but that of a student, perhaps in Paris, but more certainly at Arles in what is now south-east France. In this ancient river port, Nicholas would have lived among the remains of the ancient Roman naval base of Arelate and studied, in all likelihood, law, a subject which Arles was a famous centre for at the time. Indeed the advancement of legal knowledge was a major trend in twelfth-century Western Europe: traditional or do-it-yourself justice was increasingly being replaced by formal written law, both in the secular and religious spheres. As pope, Nicholas was able to make good use of his legal training, and even contributed new judgements to the existing body of church law.

How a poor boy like Nicholas could have got to the south coast of England, let alone the south-east of France in those days, is quite a mystery. It may be that he was subsidised by a wealthy benefactor in Hertfordshire, who sponsored the poor scholar for the good of his own soul. This would have put Nicholas under an obligation to his generous sponsor, such as that which is borne by Chaucer's Clerk of Oxenford in the *Prologue* to the *Canterbury Tales*:

But all that he might of his friends hente [get]
On books and on learning he it spent,
And busily began for the souls pray
Of them that gave him wherewith to scholeye [study]

Such a patron would surely have wanted to see some intellectual promise in the young Breakspear before he started to subsidise him, and the chances of his being a bright young scholar seem to have been slim if we believe William of Newburgh, who tells us that he couldn't even afford to go to school.

But school never was the only place to get an education. If Nicholas's father really was a priest of some kind, then it may be that he had been giving his son free Latin lessons to while away the long winter evenings by the fire. If this was the case, then Breakspear's first text-book would have been a prayer-book or Gospel-book, copied onto parchment by hand and treated as a great treasure in those days, before the invention of printing with moveable type, or the availability of cheap paper.

An early grounding in Latin would have been a marvellous start for Nicholas, since the medieval version of Latin was the language of the Christian Church in the west, used as a common language by scholars. Boso, one of Breakspear's biographers, remarks on his exceptional ability in Latin. Both Boso and William of Newburgh comment on Breakspear's intelligence and good nature, and William even says he was 'handsome of body'. This winning combination may have inspired some local sponsor to shell out the needful, to get Breakspear to the continent.

If Nicholas did not have a wealthy sponsor, it may be that he scrimped and saved for years to finance his travels, or that his family sold off some precious heirloom to give him a start in his career. In any case, as a poor wandering scholar, one of many in Europe at that time, Breakspear's outgoings would have been small, and any small acts of charity by strangers along the way would have been a great help.

At some point in his education, Nicholas might have attracted a benefice – which in those days could be a sort of ecclesiastical paid job or pension: Chaucer's Clerk is thin as a rake and wears threadbare clothes because he has not attracted any benefice, being too unworldly. Nicholas might eventually have earned extra money by acting as a tutor to more junior scholars.

III. The Abbot

If, as both Boso and William of Newburgh state, Nicholas was an adolescent when he left England, then there are quite a few 'lost' years before he became a protégé of Pope Eugenius III in the 1140s. These years are easy to account for, since a full course of study at a medieval university could take as many as twelve years to complete, if the student had both the stamina and the finances to see him through it. William of Newburgh tells us that Breakspear was a failure as a student, however, and took refuge as a canon regular at St Ruf, near Avignon. Avignon therefore became the third old Roman city, after St Albans and Arles, with which Breakspear was associated.

Avignon was to play an important role in the history of the papacy much later, in the fourteenth century, when no fewer than seven popes and two anti-popes (false claimants to the papacy) lived there between 1305 until 1378. The city, with its cold, dry mistral wind, was sold to Pope Clement VI in 1348 and remained in papal hands until 1791.

According to Bernard Gui, who wrote a

summary of Breakspear's life in the early fourteenth century, Nicholas started work for the canons of St Ruf in a priory linked to St Ruf, at a place called Melgueil. He then became a canon himself, at the mother-house of the order.

The monastery of St Ruf, outside the walls of Avignon, had been founded by four canons from the cathedral of Avignon in 1039. The occupants were called canons regular of Saint Augustine, or Austin canons, as they followed rules laid down by that saint for his community at Hippo (now Annaba in Algeria).

The Austin canons lived together under the discipline of a set rule in a monastic setting, but they were also supposed to be 'secular' priests, i.e. priests with responsibilities outside the monastery walls. Such communities, balanced between priesthood and monasticism, were well-regarded in the middle ages because, by living together under a rule, the members avoided the temptations of a life lived entirely among lay people.

In the twelfth century, the Austin canons were still quite a new feature of the church, as were the austere Cistercian or 'white monks'. Pope Eugenius III was a white monk, and a close associate of the charismatic Cistercian St Bernard of Clairvaux, who boosted the number of the order's abbeys to 338 by the time of his death in 1153.

In contrast to the Cistercians, it seems that the

canons of St Ruf, who wore soft linen cowls rather than rough woollen ones, were a pretty relaxed bunch. After several years at St Ruf, the intelligent, likeable and useful Englishman became prior; then he was elected abbot, some time around 1140.

Breakspear's duties as abbot of St Ruf obliged him to travel far to the west, to Tortosa in Catalonia. The monastery of St Ruf had dependent houses in Catalonia, but for many years the area had been under the control of the Muslim conquerors of Spain. The Muslims continued to hold parts of Spain until the late fifteenth century, but Breakspear was present when Ramon Berenguer successfully besieged the city of Tortosa in 1148.

Berenguer was a veteran of the reconquest of Almeria in south-east Spain, and, after taking Tortosa, he went on to complete the re-conquest of Catalonia by taking the cities of Fraga, Lieida and Mequinza. The so-called reconquest of Spain was seen as a crusade at this time, an enterprise equivalent to the repeated and ill-advised attempts by European armies to seize the Holy Land from the Muslims. Ramon Berenguer IV was the Count of Barcelona, and he besieged Tortosa for six months by sea and land, with help from Genoese, Flemish and English forces, as well as Templar and Hospitaller knights. At last the city fell on 30th December 1148.

The castle of La Suda, an Arab fortress that still dominates the skyline of Tortosa, served as a last refuge for the Muslim population, once the city walls had been breached.

The reconquest of Catalonia was a success that made up in some part for the embarrassing failures of the second crusade, which was still in progress when Tortosa fell. This crusade was a response to the disastrous loss of the crusader county of Edessa, an immense but thinly-populated piece of land that covered parts of what are now Turkey, Syria, Iraq and Armenia. Breakspear's patron Pope Eugenius III promoted this ill-fated crusade in a papal bull of 1145. The crusade was also preached by the aforementioned St Bernard of Clairvaux: Bernard asserted that crusaders would find redemption on the crusade – that the crusade was something like a pilgrimage, where sins could be wiped clean.

With Louis VII of France, Conrad III of Germany was one of the leaders of the second crusade. Conrad's badly-provisioned forces foolishly ignored the advice of Emperor Manuel I of Byzantium, and marched into Anatolia, where they were nearly wiped out by the Turks. Conrad was lucky to escape with his life.

King Louis took his wife, Eleanor of Aquitaine, with him on the crusade – he fared little better than Conrad. Eleanor would later marry King Henry II of England, with whom Breakspear had dealings when he was pope.

It is likely that Nicholas found time to talk to some of the English soldiers at Tortosa: they would probably have told him bloody tales of the civil war in England, which ended in the year Tortosa fell. The war was fought between the followers of King Stephen, and Matilda, the daughter of Henry I, the previous king, who had named her as his successor. Many had sworn to defend Matilda's right to the kingdom during the life of her father, but some broke their vow and went over to Stephen's side after Henry's death. The chaos caused by the war had been so terrible, the Anglo-Saxon Chronicle speculated that 'Christ and his saints were asleep'; and the historian Henry of Huntingdon asked 'Who is to bury these great throngs of dying people?'

As usually happens to some extent in any war, some people took advantage of the general disorder in Britain, using it as an excuse to raid neighbouring settlements and carry off loot. Seeing that the English state was crippled, King David of Scotland seized the opportunity to make incursions into England and to commit atrocities there. In a battle between the Norman English and the Scots, Ralph, the Bishop of the Orkneys, inspired the Normans by reminding them how many victories their nation had won not only in France and Italy, but also whilst on crusade in the Holy Land.

Breakspear's beloved St Albans played a part in the civil war when the barbaric Geoffrey de Mandeville was arrested there in 1143. Geoffrey was forced to choose between execution and the surrender of his castles – which included the Tower of London. He escaped the noose but went on to Ely, which he turned into a stronghold for himself and his band of land-pirates. He ravaged the country for miles around until he was killed at Burwell in September 1144.

Nicholas Breakspear was at Tortosa during the siege to look after the interests of his order, which went on to flourish in the newly re-conquered Catalonia. He was probably also there as a sort of unofficial papal legate. It is possible that Pope Eugenius III met Breakspear at a council held by the pope at Reims in France in the March of 1148, and sent him off to Catalonia, where the siege of Tortosa commenced three months later. If this is what happened, it was not to be the last time Eugenius would give the boy from Abbot's Langley an important job to do.

Although Abbot Nicholas Breakspear was doing great things for the canons of St Ruf in Catalonia, the canons of St Ruf at home in Provence were not altogether happy with their English abbot. They complained about him to the pope, although the precise nature of their objections to him are not known. It may be that Breakspear imposed their own rule on them a little too harshly. In any case, the pope managed to patch up the quarrel and send everyone back home to Avignon; but when the canons complained a second time, he told them to elect a new abbot, and kept Breakspear by his side.

IV. Cardinal-Bishop and Legate

The pontificate of Pope Eugenius III (born Bernardo Pignatelli) was beset with problems very similar to those that were later to afflict his protégé, Nicholas Breakspear. He spent much of his time outside Rome because of the danger posed by the volatile population. He still found time, however, to write a book about the papacy, and to show enough of his good qualities as pope to became the centre of a durable religious cult in his native Pisa, after his death. He was made a saint by Pope Pius IX in 1872.

In 1149 Eugenius made Breakspear cardinal bishop of Albano, a see in the Roman suburbs, centred on the town of the same name, which is only ten miles from Rome itself. The area is rich in Ancient Roman and early Christian history: the son of the Trojan warrior Aeneas is supposed to have founded Albano, and there was a Christian church there during the reign of the emperor Constantine, the first Roman Emperor to actively encourage Christianity. Places near Albano are also mentioned in the New Testament Book of Acts. When he was not travelling, working, or visiting Rome, Breakspear no doubt found time to inspect the cool expanse of the Lake of Albano.

The bishops of Albano had been cardinal-bishops since 1049, and before Breakspear's time their number had included men who went on to even greater things, including one who became pope (Sergius IV, 1009-12). Much as Breakspear might have enjoyed his episcopal see on the Appian Way, in 1152 his patron Eugenius III sent him as papal legate on a delicate and difficult mission to Scandinavia, where the main focus of his concern turned out to be Norway.

It is strange to think of Norway as a Catholic country, but it was indeed Catholic until the Lutheran King Christian III of Denmark and Norway succeeded in getting the Norwegians to accept Protestantism in 1539. By that time, Norway had been Christian for over three hundred years, thanks in part to the efforts of two kings called Olaf - Olaf Tryggvason (995–c.1000) and Olaf Haraldsson (1015–30).

The second of these two Olafs was made the patron saint of Norway in 1164, but he had started his career as a Viking warrior. His Viking days saw him travelling to England, Spain, and France, where he was baptised in 1013. Returning to Norway in 1015, he battled his way to the top, and became the first proper king of that country. Determined to share his new faith with his subjects, he imported English missionaries to spread the Christian gospel.

When Nicholas Breakspear, Cardinal Bishop of Albano and papal legate, arrived in 1152, the Norwegian church was, in theory, ruled from Denmark, but for years the Norwegians had been petitioning the pope for permission to have their own metropolitan. In those days, 'metropolitan' was the name for a superior Catholic bishop with responsibility for a number of dioceses: today such a person would be called an archbishop. The Norwegians thought that if they had their own metropolitan, approved by the pope, this would give their church a measure of national independence.

In Scandinavia, Breakspear was to act as *legatus a latere*, a representative of the pope sent on a special mission. As was to happen again in Breakspear's career, he arrived in the middle of a major crisis.

At that time there were three men in contention for the throne of Norway – Inge Haraldsson and his two illegitimate half-brothers, Sigurd and Eystein. If the question of which of these three should be king was not answered, Norway would descend into a civil war – and such a war would of course have made any attempt by Breakspear to reform the Norwegian church even more difficult.

Perhaps by using the charm and fluency of speech that his biographers later commented on, Breakspear won the confidence of the Norwegian courtiers and began to promote Inge as the best candidate.

Of the three, Inge was the least promising from the point of view of his physical appearance. Although he is said to have had the handsomest face of the trio, he was a hunchback who had great difficulty walking, and could neither sit a horse nor wield an axe – both useful skills for a Norwegian king in those warlike days. Some said his deformity was caused by his having been carried into a battle as a small child. Others said he had been dropped by his nurse.

Inge was a true Christian soul, full of mildness and patience, and if Breakspear achieved nothing else during his trip to Scandinavia, the election of King Inge I of Norway would have been service enough. The story of Breakspear's King Inge makes a nice contrast with Shakespeare's King Richard III, whose evil nature is reflected in his physical deformity, and whose deformity is supposed to have spurred him on to an evil life. Another difference between Inge and Richard is that, whereas Inge really was deformed, the historical Richard III is not supposed to have been deformed at all.

To their great credit, the Norwegians seem to have been able to cast aside any superstitious fear of deformity long enough to make Inge Krokrygg (meaning 'Crookback') their king, if only briefly.

As well as putting his preferred candidate on the

throne of Norway, Breakspear answered the Norwegians' prayers by establishing a metropolitan at Nidaros (now Trondheim). The first man to fill this position was John Birgersson, whose province included not only five sees in Norway, but also the Norwegian colonies on Shetland, Orkney, the Isle of Man, the Hebrides, Iceland and Greenland. Breakspear also managed to pacify the archbishops of Lund in Sweden and Bremen in Germany, both of whom believed that they should be allowed to retain their old power over the church in Norway. He even made a friend of Eskil, the archbishop of Lund, of whom more later.

V. The Leonine City

When Breakspear returned to Rome, it was the second time he had returned to that city from a successful mission abroad. In both Catalonia and Norway the Catholic Church had met with success, and word of Breakspear's having been in the right place at the right time, twice, can have done people's perception of him no harm at all.

While Breakspear had been absent in Scandinavia, Pope Eugenius III had died, as had his successor, Anastasius IV. The latter died on the third of December 1154, and the triumphant legate to Scandinavia was elected pope the very next day.

On the fifth of December Breakspear was enthroned in St Peter's church in the Leonine City, the miniature walled city connected to Rome, which contains the Vatican. Pope Leo IV had thrown a wall round this area after Rome was plundered by Muslim forces in 846. The Leonine City was outside the walls of Rome proper because St Peter's, the basilica at its heart, had been built where St Peter was thought to have been buried.

According to the list of pontiffs published in the *Catholic Encyclopedia*, Adrian IV was the one hundred and seventieth pope, and at the time of his election the papacy had been in existence for over eleven hundred years, since St Peter became the first Bishop of Rome in 32 AD.

In the early years of Christianity, the church was often persecuted by agents of the Roman Empire, but from 313 AD the Emperor Constantine began to confer privileges on followers of the new religion. The Christian emperors who succeeded Constantine had a great deal of power over the church, but this arrangement broke down after the collapse of the western part of the Roman Empire in the fifth century. That left the Bishop of Rome outside of the Roman Empire, an empire that was now based at Constantinople. When the empire fled east, the papacy found itself expanding to fit into a power vacuum. The popes became heirs not just of St Peter, but also of Constantine himself.

In the twenty-first century, the pope is the head of the world-wide Catholic church, which makes him a religious leader of unrivalled importance. He is also the head of state of a tiny country called the Vatican or Vatican City. In the twelfth century, the pope was something quite different. His power as a religious authority was limited pretty much to Western Europe, since much of the eastern Mediterranean, including Greece and what we now call Turkey, was dominated by the Byzantine Empire. This eastern empire, centred on

Constantinople, was the part of the ancient Roman Empire that was to survive until 1453. The Byzantines had their own Christian Church, now known as the Greek (or Eastern) Orthodox Church, which split off from the church in Western Europe after 1054. This historic break between the two great European churches is known as the schism of 1054, or the east-west schism.

In terms of belief and practice, the differences between the two churches in the twelfth century had to do with such things as the precise wording of the Nicene creed, the Catholic Church's use of unleavened bread in the mass, and the insistence of the Catholics on the power and authority of the pope. The division between the churches was also deepened by cultural differences between the Greek-speakers of the east and the Latin-speakers of the west.

When he was pope himself, Breakspear made a rather ham-fisted attempt to stitch up the wounds of the east-west schism, in a letter to Basil of Ochrida, Archbishop of Thessalonica. Unfortunately, Breakspear couldn't stop himself re-stating his importance as pope, and referring to the Greeks as 'lost sheep'. Basil countered that the Greeks would indeed be lost sheep if they used the version of the Nicene creed used by the Latins, and if, like the Catholics, they used unleavened bread during mass. The failure of efforts to heal the schism in the twelfth century were very much against the wishes of the Byzantine Emperor

Manuel I, who admired much about the Latin west and wanted to see an end to the schism. He also wanted to expand his own empire into the west.

While the pope's writ did not run in the east, in Western Europe and Africa his religious authority was also limited by the fact that large areas of land had been seized by Muslim forces. As we have seen, much of Spain was still dominated by the Muslims, as were some important Mediterranean islands. A further check on the influence of the pope over his church was provided by the kings and emperors of several Catholic countries and empires, who still exercised a lot of control over their local Catholic churches and resisted papal influence.

In the south of France and elsewhere, religious groups such as the Cathars or Albigensians rejected Catholic doctrine and criticised the power of the pope and of secular rulers. The Cathars, whose name came from the Greek word for 'pure', believed that Jesus was not a man at all, but an angel – an attack on the central Christian idea that Christ was incarnated as a human being. The Cathars were seen as such a threat to the authority of the Catholic church that Breakspear's successor, Pope Alexander III, launched a crusade against them.

Although his religious authority was limited, the direct political authority of a pope in the twelfth century was much greater than that exercised by the pontiff today. A large part of Italy was, at least in theory, directly ruled by the pope, a part now known to historians as the papal states. Some of these lands had been donated to the papacy by the Frankish King Pepin and his son the Emperor Charlemagne in the eighth century. These possessions contributed a lot to the wealth of the papacy, and also allowed the pontiff to raise his own armies, something that would seem very strange today. Castles and fortified cities in the papal states made up something of a protective barrier around the papal heartland of Rome itself. When the politics of the city of Rome became too unstable for safety, the popes would use their properties in the papal states as emergency bolt-holes.

As a result of the success of the first crusade, the popes enjoyed some influence in the Latin crusader states of the middle east. At their greatest extent in the twelfth century these included large areas of land on the eastern Mediterranean, around such ancient cities as Jerusalem, Acre, Tyre, Sidon, Tripoli and Antioch.

Nicholas Breakspear, or Pope Adrian IV, was now the new master of the Catholic church and of the papal states, but at the time of his election he had little control over the large part of the city of Rome that lay beyond his own Leonine City. For the new pope, the Leonine walls served not as shield against the Saracens, but as a protective barrier against the people of Rome itself. Adrian had been unanimously elected by a college of cardinal-bishops, but, unlike that of his immediate predecessor Anastasius IV, Adrian's election had not been approved by the people of Rome. For four months after his election, Adrian was unable to get to the other great papal centre of Rome, the Lateran.

The roots of this problem lay in events that unfolded a decade before Breakspear became pope. In 1143 a group of Roman citizens set up a democratic senate in Rome, which they hoped would wrest power from the papacy and the aristocrats. Giordano Pierleoni, the leader of this movement, had to defend the city from an attack by the then pope, Lucius II, in 1145. Lucius is thought to have died in this attempt to regain the city by military means.

Pierleoni was soon deposed, and Pope Eugenius III was invited back into the city. Eugenius, who had appointed Breakspear to Albano and sent him as a legate to Scandinavia, then had to deal with a far more charismatic leader of the Roman people – Arnold of Brescia.

Arnold was an Augustinian canon and prior, as Breakspear had been, but he held revolutionary ideas that set him on a collision course with the papacy. He believed that the pope, and indeed all priests, should give up their possessions and properties, and live in virtuous poverty. He was condemned as a heretic in 1141, but was reconciled to Eugenius III at Viterbo in 1145.

Eugenius made the mistake of sending Arnold on a penitential pilgrimage to Rome. When the Brescian arrived there he soon became the effective leader of the new senate, and resumed his preaching against the power of the papacy.

While Arnold of Brescia controlled Rome, the English pope, Adrian IV, could not enter the main part of the city, although he could leave Rome altogether and travel elsewhere. The fact that he could not go in a procession across Rome, from the Leonine City in the north-west to the Lateran in the south-east, meant that Adrian could not participate in certain ceremonies considered essential for him to achieve full papal status. These ceremonies could only be performed in the Lateran Basilica and the Lateran Palace. This palace in the south-east was also the pope's main residence in Rome, so Arnold and his followers were effectively keeping Adrian out of his rightful home.

Adrian ordered Arnold of Brescia out of Rome, but this order was ignored. The situation came to a head when followers of Arnold wounded an elderly cardinal in the city. Adrian's response was to place Rome under an interdict: this meant that no priest in the city could administer certain of the sacraments to any of its occupants. The forbidden ceremonies included masses, marriages and burials. This was a pretty severe measure: later, in

1208, a similar interdict was imposed by Pope Innocent III on the whole of England, during the reign of King John.

At first the Roman people resisted their fear of life without the sacraments, but as Easter drew near the temptation to yield to the new pope's demands grew stronger. At last the citizens gave in, the republic collapsed and Arnold of Brescia was banished from the city. Eventually, he was captured, tried for heresy and hanged. To prevent his body becoming a magnet for grieving admirers, it was burned and the ashes scattered in the Tiber.

To the papacy, Arnold had been a serious nuisance. To the Protestants of later generations, he was seen as one of the grandfathers of the Reformation.

Adrian was at last able to enter Rome proper. The Rome that now greeted him was of course the medieval city, which looked very different from ancient Rome or the Rome familiar to modern tourists. True, many ancient buildings, including the Colosseum, the Pantheon and several great arches were still standing, but in medieval times some of these had been adapted to new uses.

Some pagan temples and mausoleums had been converted into castles or very grand private houses, and several free-standing arches had had miniature fortresses and towers built onto them. In fact parts of Rome were then a forest of defensive towers, used as refuges by eminent families when the political situation in the city became chaotic.

In medieval times, ancient buildings that had become disused were often regarded as nothing more than quarries full of high-quality stone, which could be stripped off for use in new construction projects. Stone blocks and even ancient Roman statues were routinely burned to make lime that was then used for mortar.

During the middle ages, the centre of population within Rome's walls moved to the north-west, leaving large areas of the south and east of the city uninhabited. These areas were turned into farmland – fields full of crops inside the walls of the city.

The population of the city was always boosted by hordes of pilgrims, many of whom would have travelled from such remote places as England in order to visit the sacred sites. Much of Rome's status as a Christian centre was based on stories of miracles and martyrdoms that had happened in the city, or just outside it. The martyrdoms of St Peter and St Paul were marked by churches built over their supposed burial sites: pilgrimages to these and other important churches were supposed to wipe clean the sins of the pilgrims.

Following the fall of Arnold of Brescia, Adrian IV was able to regain the papal palace of the Lateran, and perhaps complete the ceremonies that confirmed him in his new position. These would have involved the new pope's sitting in different symbolically-important seats, reciting phrases from the Bible, throwing money into crowds of spectators and taking possession of a symbolic staff and keys. He would also have been given a red silk belt, symbolising chastity, and a purple purse containing twelve stone seals and some musk. The musk was an allusion to the idea of the Gospel spreading like a sweet smell (2 Cor: 14-16) and the seals symbolised the twelve apostles.

These dramatic ceremonies were all part of Adrian's so-called *introductio* to his Lateran Palace, and the process ended when the pope entered his private chapel, the chapel of St Lorenzo. There he would venerate certain precious relics, including the umbilical cord, foreskin and sandals of Jesus, as well as the heads of St Peter and St Paul.

Once the *introductio* ceremonies were finished, Adrian's new status as pope would have been further confirmed by the unique papal Maundy Thursday ceremonies he would now be expected to perform. These took place in the Lateran Basilica, and involved further relics, including loaves from the last supper, the blood of Jesus, and the Ark of the Covenant. Defenders of the idea that the Ark was then stored in the Lateran Church would no doubt argue that some of the contents of the Temple at Jerusalem had been brought to Rome by Titus (later emperor) in 71 AD. The Arch of Titus, that still stands in Rome, shows Roman soldiers carrying recognisable Jewish artefacts, including a menorah or seven-branched candelabrum.

As well as the supposed cache of Hebrew artefacts which played an important part in Easter ceremonies at the Lateran, there was a surprising Jewish element to some of the processions in which medieval popes participated. On certain occasions it was traditional for members of the Jewish community of Rome and other cities to present the pontiff with the Torah scrolls or Books of the Law. The pope would respond by acknowledging the importance of these ancient scriptures, but also by reminding the Jews of their blindness (as Roman Catholics then saw it) in failing to recognise the importance of Jesus, who is supposed to have fulfilled the prophecies of the Old Testament.

The pope's ceremonial use of Jewish artefacts confirmed his status not just as the heir of Jesus, St Peter and Constantine, but also as the successor to the prophets of the Israelites.

VI. Barbarossa

Arnold of Brescia had been captured for Adrian by the German King Frederick I, called Barbarossa by the Italians because of his red beard. This Barbarossa should not be confused with the sixteenth-century pirate brothers who share his nickname. Frederick Barbarossa had been crowned King of Germany in 1152, at the age of thirty. This coronation happened in the cathedral of Charlemagne's old city of Aachen, and during the ceremony Frederick sat in the spartan marble chair which is thought to have been Charlemagne's throne. This chair, on its stepped platform of stone, is still to be seen at Aachen.

Charlemagne had died an emperor, but Frederick's coronation made him nothing more than a king. Many of Germany's kings had, however, been crowned as emperors by popes: this followed the tradition started by Pope Leo III, who crowned Charlemagne on Christmas day in the year 800.

Barbarossa was on hand to capture Arnold of Brescia for Adrian because he had come to Italy to be crowned emperor. This was something Frederick's immediate predecessor, King Conrad III, had never got around to doing due to political problems at home and abroad. Frederick wanted to expand and consolidate his empire, and he saw being crowned emperor as an important step in this process.

In 1153 Barbarossa and Breakspear's patron Eugenius III had signed the Treaty of Constance, in which Eugenius promised to crown Barbarossa. In return, the German promised to help the pope against the republicans in Rome and the Normans in Southern Italy. While the citizens of Rome were a massive inconvenience to the papacy, the Normans were a very serious threat.

In the year Breakspear became pope, the Normans ruled the whole of Sicily and a large chunk of Southern Italy. In the same year, 1154, a new Norman king of Sicily was crowned. William I is known to history as 'William the Bad', and unlike his contemporaries Barbarossa, Henry II of England, Emperor Manuel of Byzantium and even the English pope, he was by no means a good-looking man. He was an ugly, powerfully-built creature with a very alarming presence.

The Italian part of William's territory ran right up to the Papal States, and was therefore an obvious threat to the papacy. Unable to repel any invasion from the south with just their own forces, both Eugenius III and Adrian IV wanted to use

Barbarossa as an ally against the Normans. While Adrian waited for news of his progress south, Barbarossa was seriously delayed on his way down to Rome to be crowned. His route to took him through Lombardy in Northern Italy, which he regarded as part of his own empire. As he passed through this prosperous region, he became involved in the struggles between its various towns and cities. In particular, ambassadors from Como, Lodi and Pavia came to Barbarossa's camp at Roncaglia and complained about the behaviour of Milan.

The army that Barbarossa had with him in Lombardy was not as large as he had originally planned for, so an attack on the city of Milan seemed impractical. Frederick decided to attack Milan's ally Tortona instead .

The Germans besieged Tortona for two months, until the wells dried up and the people were forced to surrender. Frederick evacuated the entire population and completely destroyed the little town.

Despite their lack of cannon, or explosives of any kind, European armies at this period regularly used the tactic of completely levelling an enemy settlement. If the population was spared, it was a more merciful way of concluding a siege than killing or enslaving the townspeople. The tactic also made sense strategically, as many towns and cities of the period were heavily fortified and could become a problem again if they fell into enemy hands.

It was during the last stretch of his journey south through Italy that Barbarossa seized Arnold of Brescia and handed him over to Adrian. He was then ready to meet the pope.

The first meetings between the new pope and the young German king, and the preliminaries to those meetings, contained a strong element of farce. To understand how farcical they were, we have to remember that although the audience at a farcical play is often very amused, the characters in the play itself spend a lot of their time feeling very stressed.

The pope, who was staying at Civita Castellana, sent an embassy to Frederick, and Frederick sent his own embassy to the pope at about the same time. This of course meant that each of these potentates received embassies from the other, before they had got word from their own ambassadors about how things were in the opposite camp. The embassies were sent back, but luckily bumped into each other and proceeded, together, to see Frederick.

At last the pair met in person at Campo Grasso near Sutri. In the age of television, such a politically important first meeting would probably be a carefully stage-managed encounter in front of cameras, with the participants smiling against a carefully-chosen backdrop. Certain key features, such as ritual handshakes and attempts at small talk, would be beamed around the world and watched by millions on television and via the internet.

In the twelfth century, such meetings also had a strong element of ritual, but in the case of Adrian's first encounter with Barbarossa, the preparation and stage-management left much to be desired.

What was supposed to happen was that Frederick would hold the reins of the pope's horse and lead it as far as a stone could be thrown. He was then supposed to assist the pope in dismounting by holding the pontiff's stirrup. Having dismounted, Adrian was to seat himself, and the king was to prostrate himself before the pope. Frederick was then to receive the kiss of peace from Adrian. This at least was the procedure as the papal party saw it. It may be that a failure of communication before the ritual meant that there were different expectations on each side.

Frederick led the pope's horse, but refused to hold the stirrup. As a result, when he had prostrated himself before Adrian, the pope refused to give Barbarossa the kiss of peace, explaining that he could not do so because Frederick had shown disrespect to the apostles Peter and Paul by refusing to hold his stirrup. This must have been a very frosty moment: the equivalent, in fact, of a foreign premier meeting the president of the United States and refusing to shake his hand, in front of a hundred TV cameras.

It was extremely brave of Adrian to insist on the full version of the ritual, especially when so much was riding on his ability to come to some agreement with the German king. Who else was to defend Rome against the Normans, and who else could bring the Romans themselves to heel?

After Frederick had assured himself that the full ritual was indeed traditional, and did not make him appear like a slave of the pope, the whole thing was gone through properly on the morning of the eleventh of June, 1155. This reconciliation led to a formal agreement between the papacy and the empire, confirming the terms of the Treaty of Constance and committing both parties to mutual respect and protection. In particular, neither Adrian nor Frederick were supposed to enter into any separate agreements with the Normans, the Roman senate or the Byzantine empire.

Having made and confirmed his promises, Frederick was now ready to be made an emperor, but this important ritual could not of course happen straight away, in a field. Only St Peter's Basilica would do. The problem was that the Roman senate didn't want the coronation to take place, except on their own terms. Representatives of the senate met both pope and king outside the city, where they demanded fifteen thousand pounds of silver before they would allow the coronation. Barbarossa protested that he just didn't have the money, which was probably true.

Frederick arranged for some of his soldiers to occupy the Leonine City. Very early the next morning, the pope and the king met, and the imperial coronation took place. Frederick was given a crown, sceptre and orb, and was sprinkled with oil. After this, a solemn mass was performed. The architects of this clandestine ceremony had hoped to put the citizens of Rome off the scent by holding it on a Saturday instead of a Sunday, which was more usual. The Romans soon found out, however, and numbers of them swarmed over the Tiber to attack the pope's city.

By this time, Barbarossa was outside the walls again, but he re-entered the city with his soldiers and fought to regain control. After several hours, Frederick was in charge, but over a thousand Romans were dead.

It was now June the eighteenth, 1155. Barbarossa's army, which had of course been delayed on its journey to Rome by the siege of Tortona, was reluctant to do what their leader had planned to do, which was to press further south and fight the Normans. Like many visitors from the north, they were finding the Italian summer unbearably hot, and numbers of Frederick's soldiers went down with dysentery and malaria. They began to head back north, even though an embassy from Byzantium offered Frederick a fortune to stay and fight.

VII. William the Bad

Up to the time of Barbarossa's withdrawal, Adrian IV had acted with considerable courage and decisiveness in dealing with the important challenges he faced. He had employed the harsh sanction of an interdict on Rome, and had cooperated to some extent in the execution of Arnold of Brescia. He had also stood up to Barbarossa, and in effect forced him to back down on an important matter of protocol.

The English pope had been lucky in that the interdict had worked, Arnold had been captured, and Barbarossa had participated properly in the horse-ceremony after a short delay. As the new emperor headed back to Germany, however, the pope saw his good luck, and his control of events, crossing the Brenner Pass with the Germans. He found himself stranded in exile at Tivoli, to the east of Rome. It was here that another Adrian, the Roman Emperor, had started to build his spectacular villa over a thousand years before.

Excluded from Rome, and deserted by the emperor he had hoped would protect him from the Norman threat, this must have been a low point for

Adrian. There was, however, some good news from the south-east of Italy. Some rebellious Norman barons in Apulia (*Puglia* in Italian) led by one Robert de Bassonville, had teamed up with forces from Byzantium and started to besiege towns and cities.

The Byzantine army had been sent by the eastern emperor, Manuel I Comnenus. Manuel was obsessed by the fact that parts of Italy had once been under Byzantine control, and he was prepared to take advantage of splits in the Norman camp to try to regain them.

Manuel was by all accounts tall, dark, handsome and charming. He exercised his charm on many women, who became his mistresses, while his German wife Bertha was rather neglected by her husband. Bertha, who changed her name to the more Greek-sounding Irene when she married, was the sister-in-law of Barbarossa's predecessor, the unlucky German emperor Conrad III. This alliance was part of a Byzantine-German pact against the threat posed by the Normans.

Compared to the highly sophisticated Byzantines, the people of the western empires often seemed boorish, but Manuel had an unusual enthusiasm for all things western. He introduced the knightly sport of jousting into Byzantium, and experimented with western-style armaments for his soldiers.

Despite their reputation for high culture and

advanced civilisation, the Byzantines had highly effective armies, using weapons and tactics that had been passed down to them from their Ancient Roman forebears. In their scaled armour the Byzantine knights must have looked like terrifying steel fish. They made use of the mysterious Greek fire in their battles: this was a technology that allowed them to employ something like a modern flame-thrower to beat back soldiers besieging a castle, or to set fire to the navies of any enemy foolish enough to sail within range. Greek fire is mysterious because the exact chemical composition of the liquid used, and its mode of use, are no longer known with any certainty.

At Bari in Apulia the rebel Normans and their opportunistic Byzantine allies benefited from the fact that there were many Greeks in the city, and that the native Italians resented Norman domination. Despite the arrival of a large army loyal to the Norman King William I of Sicily, the rebels continued to meet with success, and by the end of 1155 they held the north of Apulia and the whole of Campania.

Having been present at a major siege during the reconquest of Catalonia, Adrian may have viewed the Byzantine-backed rebellion against William 'the Bad' as something like a new crusade. He happily lent his support to the rebels.

While large portions of his empire were being seized by his enemies, King William lay in bed at

Palermo in Sicily, dangerously ill. To make matters worse, there was a rebellion in Sicily itself, but as the winter of 1156 turned into spring, 'The Sicilian' recovered his health, dealt diplomatically with his own island rebels, and launched a campaign against the rebels on the mainland of Italy.

First, William's army and navy 'raised the siege' of the important port city of Brindisi, on the heel of Italy. This means that they attacked the besiegers, defeating the enemy forces that were besieging the inner citadel of the town. Next, the Normans marched on Bari, where they employed the familiar tactic of reducing the entire town to rubble, in this case sparing some religious buildings. William allowed the natives, the Bariots, to evacuate before he destroyed their town.

As William's army marched north, Adrian was lodged far to the south of Rome, in the papal city of Benevento. As the Normans approached, Adrian sent most of his cardinals away to the Campania – a brave and independent gesture. He sent out his chancellor, Roland of Siena, to greet the king. Since the Byzantines, the Italians and the rebellious Normans had all failed to draw William's sting on the battlefield, it was now time for Adrian to negotiate.

Given that he had the upper hand, it is hardly surprising that the Treaty of Benevento, signed in

June 1156, awarded massive concessions to King William. The pope agreed to his dominating an enormous area of Italy, and even allowed the King of Sicily a lot of power over the church in his own domains.

VIII. Henry II

Among the favours Adrian bestowed on William the Bad was a confirmation of his role as papal legate to Sicily. This was a privilege that had been held by the Sicilian kings for nearly sixty years, since Pope Urban II had granted it to King Roger I. For William to have this privilege confirmed would have been a powerful sign of papal approval of his regime, if he hadn't exacted this concession from the pope at a time when he, the king, held all the cards.

While Adrian was still at Benevento, he was visited by a fellow countryman, John Of Salisbury. John was one of the leading scholars in England in his day, and he moved in powerful circles, among princes of both the secular and the spiritual variety.

It is said that Adrian always welcomed visitors from his home country, but John's visit was not just a friendly one. He had a rather big favour to ask of the English pope. In his book *Metalogicus*, John claims that while he was with Adrian, he persuaded the pope to give Ireland to the English king, Henry II.

This startling claim of John's raises the question,

why on earth did John of Salisbury think that the pope owned Ireland? To answer this, we have to go back more than three hundred and fifty years, to when somebody wrote a document that came to be known as the Donation of Constantine.

The verb 'wrote' may not be the right one here, since in reality the writer was creating a forgery. The Donation was supposed to be a letter written by Emperor Constantine the Great to Pope Sylvester I, the pontiff who is said to have baptised him. In the letter, among other things, the emperor grants to Sylvester and his successors 'all the western regions' (*occidentalium regionum*).

Like the story of Pope Joan, the authenticity of the Donation of Constantine was accepted for centuries, and as a result many popes regarded themselves as the rightful owners of large parts of Western Europe.

Adrian agreed to give Ireland to the King of England, and he backed up this so-called 'Donation of Ireland' with a papal bull addressed to King Henry, exhorting him the bring what amounted to Christian civilisation to the 'rude and unlettered' people of the island. This bull, called *Laudabiliter*, has been a source of great controversy among scholars, but the general consensus seems to be that, together with Adrian's original letter and the emerald ring he sent to Henry, it constituted nothing less than papal approval of an invasion of Ireland by the English king.

At the time, it seems that Ireland was divided up between many warlike kings, and that the Irish church looked, from the point of view of Rome, like a backward, corrupt, eccentric and out-of-touch institution. In issuing *Laudabiliter* and his letter, Adrian may have been showing his concern for the spiritual well-being of the Irish, but he may also have been clearing the way for greater papal influence in their country.

As it happened, when he received *Laudabiliter* in the 1150s, Henry II was too preoccupied with other things to launch an invasion of Ireland; but he dabbled in Irish affairs by backing minor invasions carried out by his allies. His own full-scale invasion did not arrive until 1171. At this time, his actions in Ireland were formally approved, and their legality confirmed, by Adrian's successor, Pope Alexander III. Alexander wrote about 'the enormities of vice with which the people of Ireland are infected' and praised Henry as 'our dearest son in Christ'. Alexander's attitude seems a little strange when we remember that Henry's prolonged quarrel with the Archbishop of Canterbury, Thomas Becket, had led to that saint's martyrdom in the previous year.

Henry II's 1171 invasion of Ireland was an example of the use of an ostentatious military force to cow the enemy into submission without any battles being fought. The King of England crossed the Irish Sea with four hundred ships and perhaps four thousand men at his back. As well as knights and archers, the ships contained masses of food, and equipment for sieges, including siege towers. Unfortunately for Henry, the understandings he subsequently reached with the Irish kings didn't last long after he had crossed back to England.

Adrian's gift of Ireland to King Henry II might have been motivated by the pope's own warm feelings for his native country and his respect for its young king. Adrian's nostalgia for his place of birth also prompted him to to shower all sorts of privileges on St Albans Abbey, the mighty Norman house that was finished when Adrian was still just plain Nicholas Breakspear of Abbot's Langley.

Even Adrian's choice of name at his election may have been inspired by his feelings for St Albans, as some thought that, in the eighth century, the first pope called Adrian had endowed the abbey with special privileges.

Adrian may have had personal family reasons for favouring St Albans as he did, as it is likely that his father, Richard, was still living in the abbey when Adrian was pope. Richard was buried under the chapter house along with several abbots – a great honour.

In a series of letters to England, Adrian ensured that St Albans became independent, wealthy, powerful and privileged. Though ruled by an abbot, it would not have to defer to any local bishop, and Adrian made sure that it was able to detach itself from the influence of the Bishop of Lincoln, whose power over the abbey had been resented by the abbot. The only bishop St Albans had to answer to was the pope himself, and the abbot was allowed to wear certain items that were usually reserved for bishops or popes, including a mitre and sandals. Like the Donation of Ireland to Henry II, Adrian's favours shown to St Albans were confirmed by his successor, Alexander III.

As well as an understandable regard for the county of his birth, the special favours Adrian granted to St Albans were no doubt inspired by his veneration for St Alban himself, who is supposed to have been martyred in the city that now bears his name, early in the fourth century.

The legend tells us that Alban was a pagan living in the Roman city that was then called Verulamium. He sheltered a refugee from the persecution of the Christians at that time, was then converted by the man and underwent baptism. When the governor's men came to search Alban's house for the fugitive, Alban put on his cloak and pretended to be the one they sought. As a result, Alban was scourged and then killed, but not before he had stopped a river flowing while he crossed it, and converted his executioner to Christianity. Finding that he could not kill such a fine member of the Christian community he had just joined, the headsman had to be replaced by another man, who was struck blind after he had done the job. A spring miraculously appeared where Alban was beheaded.

With Frederick Barbarossa, William the Bad and Manuel Comnenus of Byzantium, Henry II of England was one of the four powerful, ambitious and rather young European rulers with whom Pope Adrian IV had dealings during his pontificate. In 1154, the year of Adrian's coronation, William was the oldest, at thirty-four, and Henry, at only twenty-one, was the youngest. Both William and Henry were crowned in the year of Adrian's election.

Although only Frederick and Manuel were actually called 'Emperor', the title could just as easily have been applied to the other two. At his coronation, Henry II already ruled Normandy, Anjou, Maine, Touraine, Aquitaine, Poitou and Auvergne; which together made up the so-called 'Angevin Empire', a hefty slice of the north-west of France. As we have seen, William ruled Sicily and most of mainland Italy south of Rome.

IX. Barbarossa Returns

In signing the treaty of Benevento with William the Bad, Adrian was in contravention of the Treaty of Constance which Eugenius III had signed with Barbarossa, and which Adrian himself had confirmed. The diplomatic situation between emperor and pope was now like a tinder-dry wooden house on a hot, rainless day. All that was needed was a spark to set the whole thing alight.

The unsuspecting source of ignition was the aforementioned Eskil, Archbishop of Lund in Sweden. Eskil, who was probably of an age with Adrian, had got to know the pope when he was papal legate to Scandinavia. When he heard of his old friend's assumption of the chair of Peter, Eskil made the long journey to Rome to pay his respects. On his way back he was kidnapped and held to ransom in Germany.

Whether Barbarossa had a hand in this kidnapping is open to question. It may be that Barbarossa didn't like Eskil because he was friends with Adrian, and was associated with Breakspear's time in Scandinavia, when among other things the legate had tried to isolate the Scandinavian churches from the control of Germany. Even if Barbarossa didn't have anything to do with the original kidnapping, he seems to have made a point of not exactly rushing to the aid of the hapless hostage.

Adrian sent a letter of complaint about this to Barbarossa, who was holding court at Besançon, in what is now Eastern France, in September 1157. Frederick's beautiful but very young new wife, Beatrix, had a claim to lands in this area, which included the then ill-defined region of Burgundy.

This Besançon court or diet was supposed to be a very impressive event. There were ambassadors from all over Western Europe, but the ambassadors from the pope had not been sent to venerate the imperial bridegroom or to add to his prestige.

When Adrian's letter of complaint was read to Barbarossa and his followers, the match was well and truly put to the tow. Adrian reminded the emperor that he himself had given him the crown of the empire as a gift. He added that he wished he could have given him more gifts, or *beneficia* in Latin.

It was the word *beneficia*, or the way that it was translated for Barbarossa, that caused the trouble. Taken one way, *beneficium* could mean a simple gift or, in this case, Adrian's simple action of placing a crown on the head of an emperor. Taken another way, *beneficium* could suggest that Adrian thought the empire was his (Adrian's) by right, and that he had chosen to give it to Barbarossa for safe keeping. The second interpretation cast Barbarossa as something like a poor knight who has been given some land in return for services rendered to his feudal lord. This, Barbarossa could not tolerate.

It seems that Barbarossa's henchmen, assembled at Besançon, immediately took the word *beneficia* to mean that Adrian was suggesting Barbarossa was a feudal vassal to the pope. There was instant uproar, and Barbarossa's close associate Otto von Wittelsbach, Count Palatine of Bavaria, unsheathed his sword and lunged at the papal ambassadors. Barbarossa himself was forced to intervene to prevent bloodshed. The ambassadors, who included the future Pope Alexander III, were sent home with a flea in their collective ear. Poor Eskil, the Archbishop who had unintentionally started all this trouble, was not released by his kidnappers until 1158.

Later, Adrian chose to calm the situation by sending another letter to Barbarossa, explaining that by *beneficia* he had indeed meant simple gifts, or good deeds. By the time this second letter arrived, Barbarossa had already embarked on his second expedition to Italy.

The German emperor had his eye on the prosperous Northern Italian region of Lombardy, which he regarded as a part of his empire that needed to be reclaimed. Barbarossa's plan was a complex new version of an old favourite – divide and rule. The political crack in Lombardy, where Barbarossa hoped to insert his military crow-bar, was the continuing animosity between Milan and the cities loyal to Milan, and the smaller cities that felt oppressed by Milan.

When Barbarossa first entered Lombardy in 1155, he had already been aware of these divisions, but at that time he thought it unwise to try to besiege Milan itself – as we have seen, he attacked Milan's ally Tortona instead. In 1158, an all-out siege of Milan seemed practical, and this is what Barbarossa began. The siege occupied much of August 1158, and heat and disease took its toll both on the besieged and their besiegers. At last a peace was signed, and Milan became an imperial city.

During the siege the Bishop of Ravenna died, on the twelfth of August. The bishop had been a loyal friend of Barbarossa, and approved of the emperor's attack on Milan. Not surprisingly, Barbarossa wanted to replace him with another supporter, and he engineered the election of one Guido, son of his friend Count Guido of Biadrante, even though this young man was not yet in holy orders. The pope objected to this. He also objected to Frederick's interference in a dispute between the cities of Bergamo and Brescia, the settlement of which had been confirmed by papal legates in 1158. Adrian was also unhappy about the kidnapping of two of his papal envoys and, on a larger scale, about the whole business of Barbarossa riding into Italy and subduing cities.

Adrian resented Barbarossa's expansionist plans in Italy partly because he himself wanted to extend his influence in the peninsula and beyond. During his pontificate, Adrian laid claim to Spoleto, Ferrara, Sardinia, Corsica and parts of Tuscany. Soon after his election, the new pope sent an army to besiege the castle of Acquapuzza, which was reclaimed for the papacy in September 1158. Acquapuzza was a *castra*, or fortified town, as were other places Adrian acquired. Many of these were in positions which enabled them to watch over important roads and approaches to Rome itself. In claiming such places near to Rome, Adrian was acting like his eighth-century namesake, Pope Adrian I.

As well as regions, cities and towns, pope and emperor also disagreed about certain petty things that had, for them at least, a powerful symbolic meaning. Adrian had sent an important message to Barbarossa via an 'unworthy messenger – a lowly fellow', which was taken as an insult. Barbarossa responded to Adrian's failure to cooperate in the election of Guido by insisting that his (the emperor's) name be placed above the pope's in any official letters he sent out.

Both Barbarossa and Adrian conspired with each other's enemies. Adrian gave direct encouragement to Milan even before Barbarossa started to lay siege to it, and later, in the August of 1159, the pope hosted a meeting between representatives of the Lombard cities and William I of Sicily, at Anagni. Meanwhile Frederick sent his representative Otto von Wittelsbach to Rome to try to arrange some sort of pact against Adrian with the Roman senate.

At this moment of tension, with escalation and conspiracy in the air, Pope Adrian IV, otherwise known as the Englishman Nicholas Breakspear, died, on 1st September 1159. He was probably about 59 years old, and had been pope for four years, six months and twenty-eight days.

X. Pope and Anti-Pope

There are differing views about what actually killed Adrian IV. Some say angina, but other authors tell us that the culprit was quinsy; or a fly that stuck in his throat when he was drinking some wine. Angina, which is a narrowing of the arteries, is entirely consistent with a man approaching sixty, who was suffering from stress, took little exercise and, perhaps, enjoyed a rich diet.

Quinsy, which doctors now call peritonsillar abscess, is a swelling of the area around the tonsils, which can restrict breathing. These days, the condition is rare, and usually appears among children and young adults. It is entirely possible that Adrian suffered from both angina and quinsy, and that he also inhaled a fly that went down the wrong way. If that happened to a man whose health was already severely compromised, it seems more likely that the fly in the wind-pipe would prove fatal. We should also bear in mind that, in twelfth-century Europe, fifty-nine was a very ripe old age that few men and even less women could seriously hope to reach. It is likely that, as a very old man by medieval standards, Adrian had other health problems that contemporary chroniclers never bothered to mention.

When news of the pope's death reached Rome, Barbarossa's agent Otto von Wittelsbach was still there trying to turn the people of the city against Adrian. Now that a new pope had to be elected, Otto set about engineering the election of a pontiff who would be sympathetic to Barbarossa, his German empire and its expansionist plans.

Otto's scheme was frustrated because many of the cardinals who were qualified to elect the next pope wanted to honour the terms of the agreement Adrian had come to at Anagni with the Lombards and the Normans. The parties at Anagni had agreed to continue to support each other against the Germans even after Adrian's death. The result was that the majority of cardinals voted for Cardinal Roland Bandinelli, who had been Adrian's trusted chancellor. It was Cardinal Roland who had confronted Barbarossa with the controversial *beneficia* letter at Besançon in 1157, and who had had a sword brandished at him by the same Otto von Wittelsbach who was now working against him in Rome.

Fourteen cardinals voted for Roland, who took the papal name of Alexander III. Nine chose Cardinal Ottaviano, a prelate sympathetic to Barbarossa. Ottaviano did not choose to accept his defeat with a philosophical shrug of the shoulders.

Instead he waited until the papal robe had been put on Alexander, then snatched it off and put it on himself. A senator, wading into this undignified mêlée, snatched the robe back for Alexander, but then Ottaviano's followers brought out a spare robe they had brought along. Ottaviano then proceeded to put this extra robe on upside-down and back-to-front, which was seen as a very bad omen.

Ottaviano took the name of Victor IV, and his followers locked up the 'real' pope, Alexander, for twelve days. Victor was able to live as pope in Rome because he had the support of the Roman people and of Barbarossa. Many, however, regarded him as an anti-pope.

While Victor remained in Rome, Alexander lived in exile, mainly in France. Barbarossa continued to support a string of anti-popes until 1177, when he finally recognised Alexander III as the true heir of St Peter.

Barbarossa died in 1190 at the age of sixty-seven. He drowned while trying to cross the Saleph river in Armenia. This was during the Third Crusade, which had set out to free Jerusalem from the army of Saladin. There is, however, a medieval legend to the effect that Barbarossa is not dead at all, but sleeps, sitting upright at a table, deep inside the Kyffhäuser Mountain in Thuringia. His strong red beard has now grown right through the table but Barbarossa is still waiting, biding his time until he returns to re-establish the German empire.

By contrast, Pope Adrian IV, the only English pope, lies in a third-century granite coffin below St Peter's basilica in Rome. In his tomb he wears Turkish slippers, dark silk robes and an emerald ring.

XI. Conclusion – John of Salisbury

It was the English scholar John of Salisbury who managed to extract from Adrian IV his blessing on a future invasion of Ireland by Henry II. While he was with the pope in Italy, John and Adrian had some frank discussions about the papacy which John recorded in his book *Policraticus*.

John boldly related to his countryman the pope some of the objections to the church in general, and the papacy in particular, that were then current in Western Europe. His most serious charge was that, while idle senior clerics grew rich, many of the common people remained poor. This situation, John implied, was made worse by the fact that the poor themselves financed the luxury in which the princes of the church lived.

In answer to this charge, Adrian recounted an old story, the fable of the belly. The gist of this story is that, once upon a time, all the different parts of the body rebelled against the stomach. They objected that, whereas they, the hands and feet, etc. did all the work, the stomach got all the food. The rebellious body-parts refused to cooperate in supplying food to the belly, but of course they soon found that they all suffered, since the belly was now no longer able to supply them with the nourishment they all shared. The moral of the story is that powerful people need to be richly rewarded because everyone else depends on them.

Even a cursory glance at this fable will reveal that it cannot justify rich rewards for powerful people, as the belly has to redistribute the goodness it gains, while rich and powerful people often find ways to avoid this.

There is no record of John of Salisbury pouring scorn on the pope's use of this fable. The chances are that John had already come across the story in the works of the first-century Greek writer, Plutarch. In Plutarch's biography of the Roman general Coriolanus, the fable is used by a senator called Menenius to calm a rebellious Roman mob.

Shakespeare wrote a play about this same Coriolanus, and made use of the fable of the belly. There is, therefore, a link between Breakspear and Shakespeare, the other Roman Catholic Englishman we think of when we read Breakspear's name. Shakespeare used a sixteenth-century English translation of Plutarch, and may even have encountered the fable in Camden's *Remaines*, a history book published in 1605. From page 198 of his *Remaines*, Camden very briefly tells the story of the English pope, using John of Salisbury's *Policraticus* as his source. Much of

Camden's short account of the career of Breakspear is taken up with a version of the fable of the belly.

As well as reminding John of old fables, Adrian confided to the man from Salisbury that he was having a rotten time as pope. He told him that the pontiff's throne is a 'prickly seat', that his garments are sewn together with thorns and that the mitre might as well be fashioned out of fire. In a remarkably intimate confession, Adrian admitted that he wished himself back in England, or at Avignon.

One can certainly see Adrian's point: during his short pontificate Italy was plagued by wars and invasions, and as pope he had to deal with ambitious and unscrupulous men with armies much bigger than his own. This is one way to view the pontificate of England's only pope – as a time when the pontiff was forced to ride out a prolonged political and military storm. Adrian's response to this endless grappling for land and power was to expand and consolidate his own sphere of influence as much as possible, and then to deal with external threats as best he could.

After a few decisive actions that paid off at the beginning of his pontificate, Adrian was forced to bend with the wind after Barbarossa deserted him in the summer of 1155. Throughout, he showed a chameleon quality in his dealings with different people and events - sometimes he would present himself as a friend or even a loving father to the powers he had to deal with – at other times he acted as a fellow-conspirator, and at times as a stern judge, deploying his army or wielding the terrible threat of excommunication or interdict. The depressing thing about all the conflicts Adrian had to cope with is that they had been going on for generations before Adrian ascended the throne of Peter, and would continue for generations afterwards.

Adrian didn't spend all his time as pope securing power and playing his enemies off against each other, however. We have seen how he conferred great advantages on the abbey of St Albans in his home county of Hertfordshire, a programme inspired not just by local patriotism, but also by what seems to have been a genuine reverence for England's first Christian martyr, St Alban.

The English pope also made reforms within the papacy, and in one notable case reinforced an important aspect of church law. To understand this action of Adrian's, we must remember that in the Europe of the twelfth century many people were 'un-free', although technically they were not actually slaves. These were the millions of serfs and peasants who were bound to the land they tilled, and were utterly under the control of their masters within the hierarchy of the feudal system.

As pope, Adrian was asked to make a judgement on whether a proper Christian marriage between two such un-free people could legally be dissolved by their feudal master, if he did not approve of the match. To his great credit, Adrian insisted that, even in the face of such opposition, a Christian marriage could not be dissolved, and that the otherwise powerless bride and groom could remain married. This was one in the eye for the feudal lords, and a great gesture in favour of love.

During his short pontificate, the English pope continued with the reform agenda that had been championed by the eleventh century Pope Gregory VII. Gregory was so active in the cause of reform that the eleventh century reforms of the western church are known as the Gregorian Reforms. Gregory was concerned to ensure the independence and authority of the papacy, and to decrease the influence of secular rulers over church affairs. He insisted that lay people, even if they were kings, princes or emperors, should not appoint anyone to an ecclesiastical position, and that nobody should be able to commit the sin of simony by buying such an office.

Like Adrian IV, Gregory VII's policies set him on a collision course with the German emperor, in his case Henry IV. Like that between Adrian and Barbarossa, the dispute between Gregory and Henry went on for years. Gregory even excommunicated Henry three times. Henry also set up an antipope in opposition to Gregory, as Barbarossa did against Adrian's successor Alexander III.

Henry invaded Rome in 1084, but was driven out by the approach of Gregory's allies, the Normans. Robert Guiscard, Duke of Apulia and the leading Norman in Italy at the time, was the great-uncle of Adrian's Norman ally, William I. Like Adrian, Gregory died in exile, in his case at the castle of Salerno in the Campania.

As we have seen, the struggles between the pope and powerful secular rulers were not new in Adrian's time, and continued for a long time after his death. Many of these power-struggles between the Holy See and the lords of the earth centred around papal elections and attempts to put up anti-popes to knock down properly-elected popes. It is partly because of this history of external meddling that modern popes are now elected in strict secrecy, in conditions where there is virtually no contact with the outside world. But it was a long time after Nicholas Breakspear's short pontificate before the pope's electors could enjoy the luxury of a secret ballot behind locked doors, with nothing but smoke-signals to keep the world informed.

XII. Chronology

1039: Monastery of St Ruf founded at Avignon.

1054: East-West Schism.

1060: The Normans invade Sicily.

1084: Emperor Henry IV of Germany attempts to invade Rome.

1090: Birth of St Bernard of Clairvaux.

c.1100?: Birth of Nicholas Breakspear. Birth of Arnold of Brescia.

1115: Completion of St Albans Abbey.

1120: Birth of William I of Sicily.

c.1122: Birth of Byzantine Emperor Manuel I Comnenus.

c.1123: Birth of Frederick I Barbarossa.

1133: Birth of Henry II of England.

c.1140 Breakspear becomes Abbot of St Ruf.

1141: Arnold of Brescia condemned as a heretic.

1143: Democratic senate set up in Rome under Giordano Pierleoni. Papal forces attack the city under Pope Lucius II. Manuel I Comnenus becomes Byzantine Emperor.

1145: Pope Eugenius III promotes the Second Crusade in a papal bull. Arnold of Brescia and the pope are reconciled.

1148: Pope Eugenius III meets Breakspear at Reims?

1148: Siege of Tortosa, Catalonia.

1149: Breakspear becomes Cardinal-Bishop of Albano.

1152: Breakspeare sent as papal legate to Scandinavia. Barbarossa crowned King of Germany at Aachen.

1153: Death of St Bernard of Clairvaux. Barbarossa and Eugenius III sign the Treaty of Constance.

1154: Breakspear becomes Pope Adrian IV.

William I of Sicily and Henry II of England crowned.

1155: Barbarossa meets Pope Adrian IV. Probable date of execution of Arnold of Brescia.

1156: Treaty of Benevento: Adrian IV and William I.

1157: Adrian sends *beneficium* letter to Barbarossa.

1158: Barbarossa's siege of Milan.

1159: Adrian hosts Lombard/Sicily meeting at Anagni. Death of Adrian. Pope Alexander III elected. Victor IV supported as Anti-Pope by Barbarossa.

1166: Death of William I of Sicily.

1171: Henry II of England invades Ireland.

1180: Death of Manuel I Comnenus.

1189: Death of Henry II of England.

1190: Death of Frederick I Barbarossa.

XIII. Bibliography

Almedingen, Edith M.: *The English Pope (Adrian IV)*, Heath Cranton, 1925

Baumgartner, Frederic J.: *Behind Locked Doors: A History of the Papal Elections*, Palgrave, 2003

Bede: *The Ecclesiastical History of the English People*, Oxford, 2008

Bolton, Brenda and Duggan, Anne J: *Adrian IV the English Pope (1154-1159) Studies and Texts*, Ashgate, 2003

Burn, Robert: *Ancient Rome*, George Bell and Sons, 1895

Chaucer, Geoffrey: *The Canterbury Tales*, Oxford, 1906

Cheetham, Nicholas: *Keepers of the Keys: The Pope in History*, Macdonald, 1982

Collins, Roger: *Keepers of the Keys of Heaven: A*

History of the Papacy, Weidenfeld & Nicholson, 2009

Comnena, Anna: *The Alexiad*, Routledge and Kegan Paul, 1967

Deanesly, Margaret: A History of the Medieval Church: 590-1500, Methuen, 1954

Frothingham, Arthur L.: *The monuments of Christian Rome*, Macmillan, 1908

Henry of Huntingdon: *The History of the English People 1000-1154*, Oxford, 2002

Hetherington, Paul: *Medieval Rome: a Portrait of the City and its Life*, Rubicon, 1994

Kendall, Alan: *Medieval Pilgrims*, Wayland, 1970

Morris, Colin: *The Papal Monarchy*, Oxford, 1989

Munz, Peter: *Frederick Barbarossa: A Study in Medieval Politics*, Eyre & Spottiswoode, 1969

Norwich, John Julius: *Byzantium: The Decline and Fall*, Viking, 1995

Norwich, John Julius: *The Kingdom in the Sun 1130-1194*, Longman, 1970

Poole, A.L.: *Domesday Book to Magna Carta*, Oxford, 1955

Royidis, Emmanuel: *Pope Joan*, Deutsch, 1954

Runciman, Steven: *The Eastern Schism*, Oxford, 1955

Shakespeare, William: *Coriolanus*, Methuen, 1976

Tout, T.F.: *The Empire and the Papacy 918-1273*, Rivingtons, 1921

Warren, W.L.: *Henry II*, Eyre Methuen, 1973

www.ingramcontent.com/pod-product-compliance
Lightning Source LLC
Chambersburg PA
CBHW070355271224
19534CB00029B/202